HALF SQUARE TRIANGLES
Exploring Design

Barbara Johannah, P.O. Box 396, Navarro, CA 95463

HALF SQUARE TRIANGLES
EXPLORING DESIGN

BARBARA JOHANNAH

© 1987 Barbara Johannah

Cover by Charlotte Patera
Novato, Ca

Text and most of the drawings were done on an
Apple Macintosh Computer

Color Photography by E. Z. Smith
Fresno, Ca

except as listed below
photos of Pat Cairn's work submitted by the artist
Enchanted Hill and Oahu by the artist
Garden of Eden by the artist

Black & White Photography by Vagt Photography
Ukiah, Ca

except page 43
Kurt Bjorkquist

Front Cover Photo by Laura Julienne
Albion, CA

Thank you for your help
Vern, Miriam, David, Clint,
Judy, Gwen, & Kirsten
Todd of Ukiah Computer Center
everyone at the Green Mac
Janet of e & j computer graphics
Ling of Copy Plus

Published by
Barbara Johannah
PO Box 396
Navarro, CA 95463

ISBN: 0-934342-04-0

All rights reserved. No part of this work covered by the
copyright hereon may be reproduced or used in any
form or by any means-graphic, electronic, or mechanical,
including photocopying, recording, taping or information
storage and retrieval systems without written permission of
the publisher.

Printed in the United States of America

This book is based on the design exploration fun of

Jane Warnick

Sometimes the voice speaking is Jane's and sometimes it is mine.

Barbara Johannah

PURPOSE OF THE BOOK

To systematize the process of discovering half square triangle patterns of which there are an infinite number and to place these patterns within quick piecing methods.

CONTENTS

1. History _____ 11
    Introduction _____ 11
        The System According to Douat _____ 12
        The System According to Warnick _____ 13
2. The Half Square Triangle Element Key _____ 14
3. Pattern Formation _____ 16
    Translation _____ 16
    Rotation _____ 17
    Reflection _____ 24
    Combination _____ 26
    Borders _____ 28
    Rubic's Cube _____ 30
4. Methods of Approach _____ 32
    Graph Paper _____ 32
    Carved Stamp _____ 35
    Fabric _____ 42
    Copy Machine _____ 46
    Computer _____ 49
5. Logical Break-up _____ 50
6. Method of Sewing _____ 53
        Half Square Triangles _____ 54
        Quarter Square Triangles _____ 56
        Squares _____ 60
7. Instant Gratification _____ 64
    Artists _____ 79

HISTORY

INTRODUCTION

The journey begins in the early 18th century with a French Monk named Dominique Douat. Fascinated with the designs that could be made with light and dark half square triangles, Douat worked with tiles to find all possible design variations within a given framework. He then worked out the infinite system of design which could be created from the original possibilities. The Royal Academy of Sciences in Paris published a paper in 1704 on this infinite system of design which Douat devised. In 1979 E. H. Gombrich presented several illustrations and a mention of Douat's system in his book, THE SENSE OF ORDER (70-72). Almost 300 years after Dominique Douat originally made his discoveries, Jane Warnick came across these pages about Douat's work. She was immediately struck with the applicability of the system to quilt design. The photos from Douat's book, which Gombrich presented, looked like quilts just waiting to be made. Since she had used Ernest Haight's and Barbara Johannah's methods of piecing half square triangles, she knew that putting these quilts together would be simple and fast. That very evening Jane began an exploration of the system which has fascinated her ever since.

DOMINIQUE DOUAT

JANE WARNICK

ERNEST HAIGHT

BARBARA JOHANNAH

Jane adapted the system to quilt patterns and developed The Half Square Triangle Element Key. In the book you will learn various ways of manipulating the Elements in the Key to discover an unlimited number of half square triangle patterns and to place these patterns within quick piecing methods. An infinite number of patterns exist within the system which only await discovery. Quiltmakers of the past have already discovered hundreds of them, Yankee Puzzle, Hopscotch, Anna's Choice, Pinwheels, and most of the star patterns just to name a few. Throughout this book you will find drawings of traditional quilt blocks which have been used to illustrate the particular operation or point being made. The new patterns, as they are recorded, will build on the traditions which the original quiltmakers began and will allow quiltmakers of today to add to the wealth of designs which our predecessors set down.

The first time Jane told Barbara about her discovery of Douat's system and of her adaptation of it to quiltmaking, Barbara suggested that Jane should write a book about it. For three years Jane kept that thought in the back of her head. In 1982 Jane suggested a collaboration believing that the method of piecing was as important to the finished quilt as was the discovery process. After several months of work, both Jane and Barbara experienced serious reverses in their lives. Now, four years later, Jane and Barbara are both doing fine. Jane has gone on to other interests. Barbara has completed this book. Quilts can be quick, but the books about them can be sloooow!

THE SYSTEM ACCORDING TO DOUAT

Pere Douat divided the square in half along the diagonal, coloring one half white and one half black. There are four possible permutations which exist, labeled A, B, C, and D. If you combine two of these, there are sixteen possible combinations. If you combine three permutations, you have 64 possibilities; and if you combine four, you have 256 possibilities. Douat placed these in a line which you can see in the photos from his book

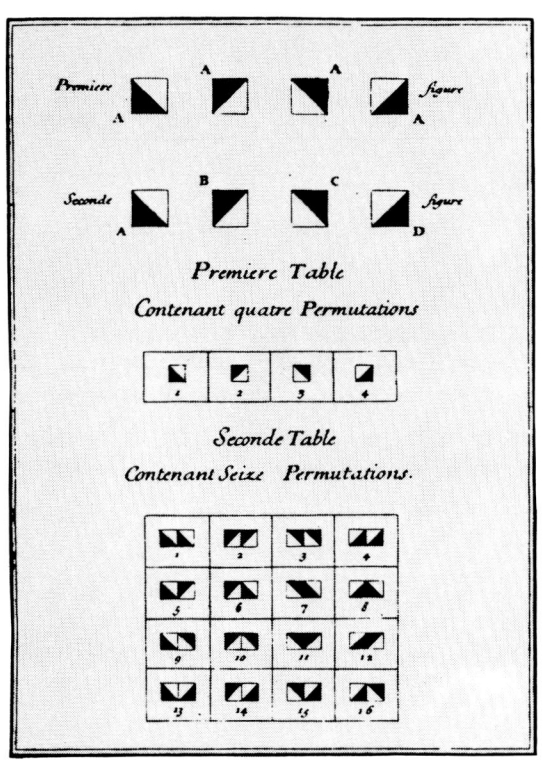
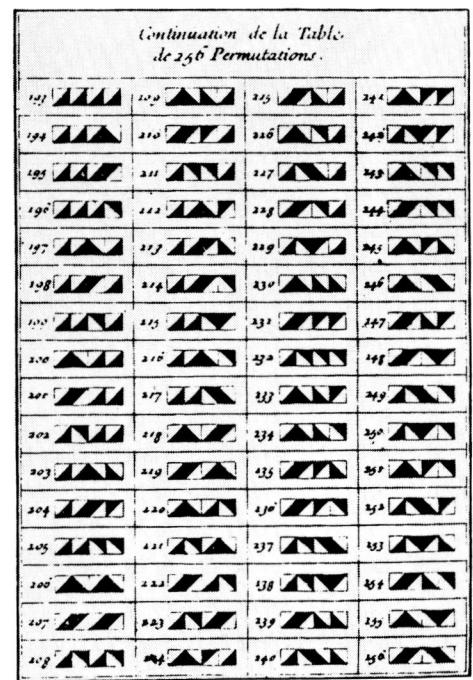

I chose to place the permutations in groups of four, as these seemed easier to relate to existing quilt blocks. These 256 elements are presented on pages 14 and 15. They are the key to the system. If you combine two of these elements, you have 65,536 possibilities. If you combine four, you have over 4 billion possibilities. All of these possibilities exist before you begin to manipulate the basic element, to add color and texture, to choose the set - in other words before you begin to design a quilt.

The key is numbered, quite arbitrarily, for two reasons. First, I needed a way to keep track of which elements I used to generate the patterns, thus avoiding repetitions. I did not want to continually cover the same ground when an infinite number of possibilities lay ahead. I also did not want to second-guess myself as to which elements I felt would generate "better" patterns to the exclusion of treasures which were surely hidden in "less promising" elements. Also, I could ask someone for an important date in her life, select the four elements which represented that date (2/20/19/46) and present the person with a unique block to use as raw material in designing a quilt.

THE SYSTEM ACCORDING TO WARNICK

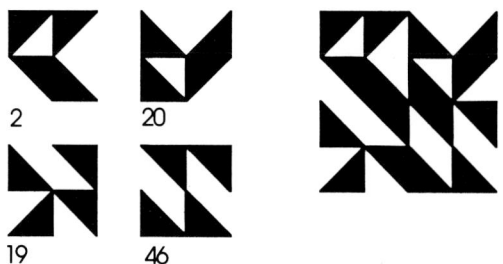

(Every day since 1/1/1 A.D. can be immortalized without ever going beyond #99 on the Key!) I have found that initial blocks selected with just 2 elements, arranged as shown, yield viable patterns with fewer operations. Thus, if your important day is June 23, 1982, you would select 6 and 23, 6 and 82 or 23 and 82. These blocks are the raw material which you will use in designing quilts and quilt blocks.

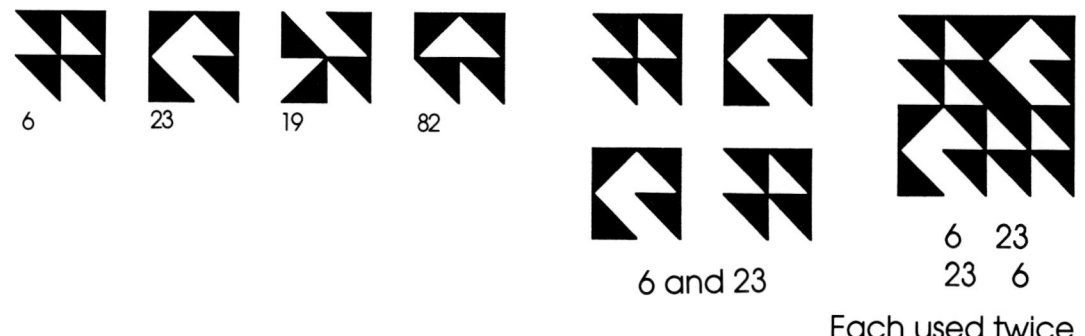

THE HALF SQUARE TRIANGLE

ELEMENT KEY

PATTERN FORMATION

TRANSLATION Translation is the repetition of a design element along an established network. There are three networks which apply: Square, Half-Drop and Brick.

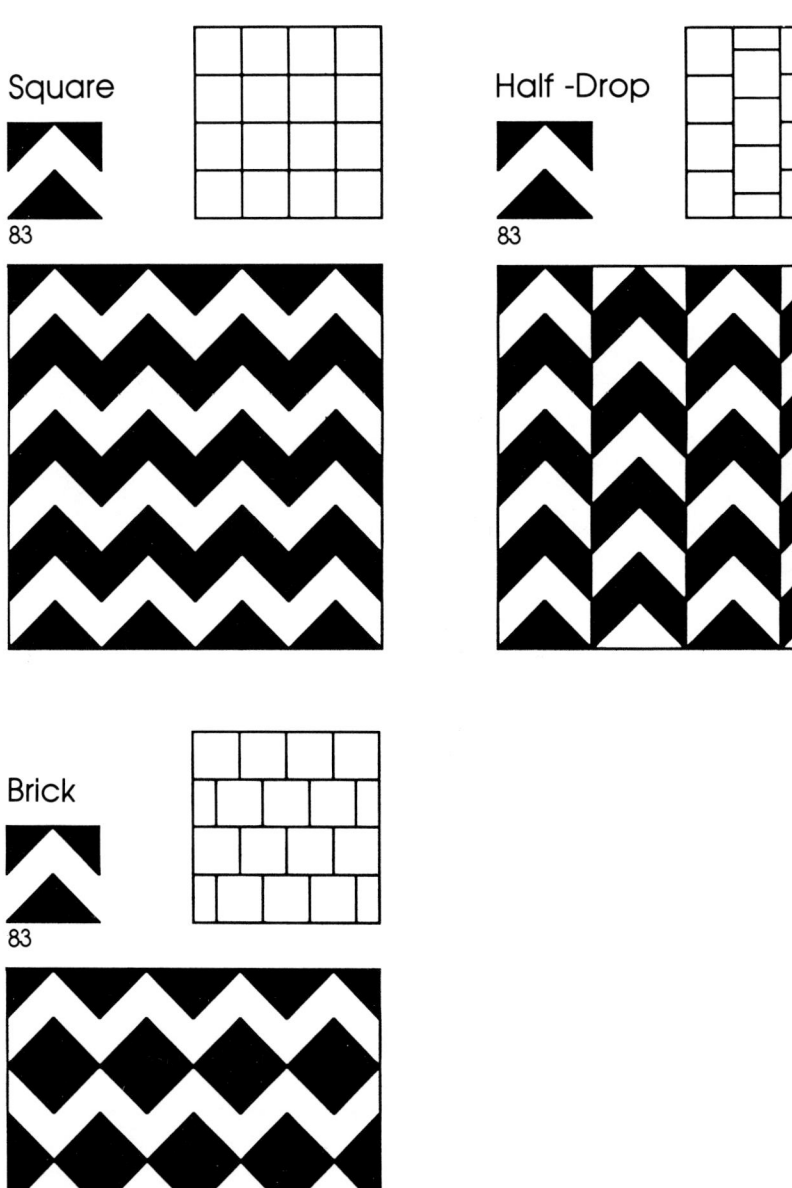

Rotation is the result of taking the design element and turning it one-quarter at a time through the square. You designate one corner of the design element as point "A" and place this point at the center of a square equal to four design elements.

ROTATION

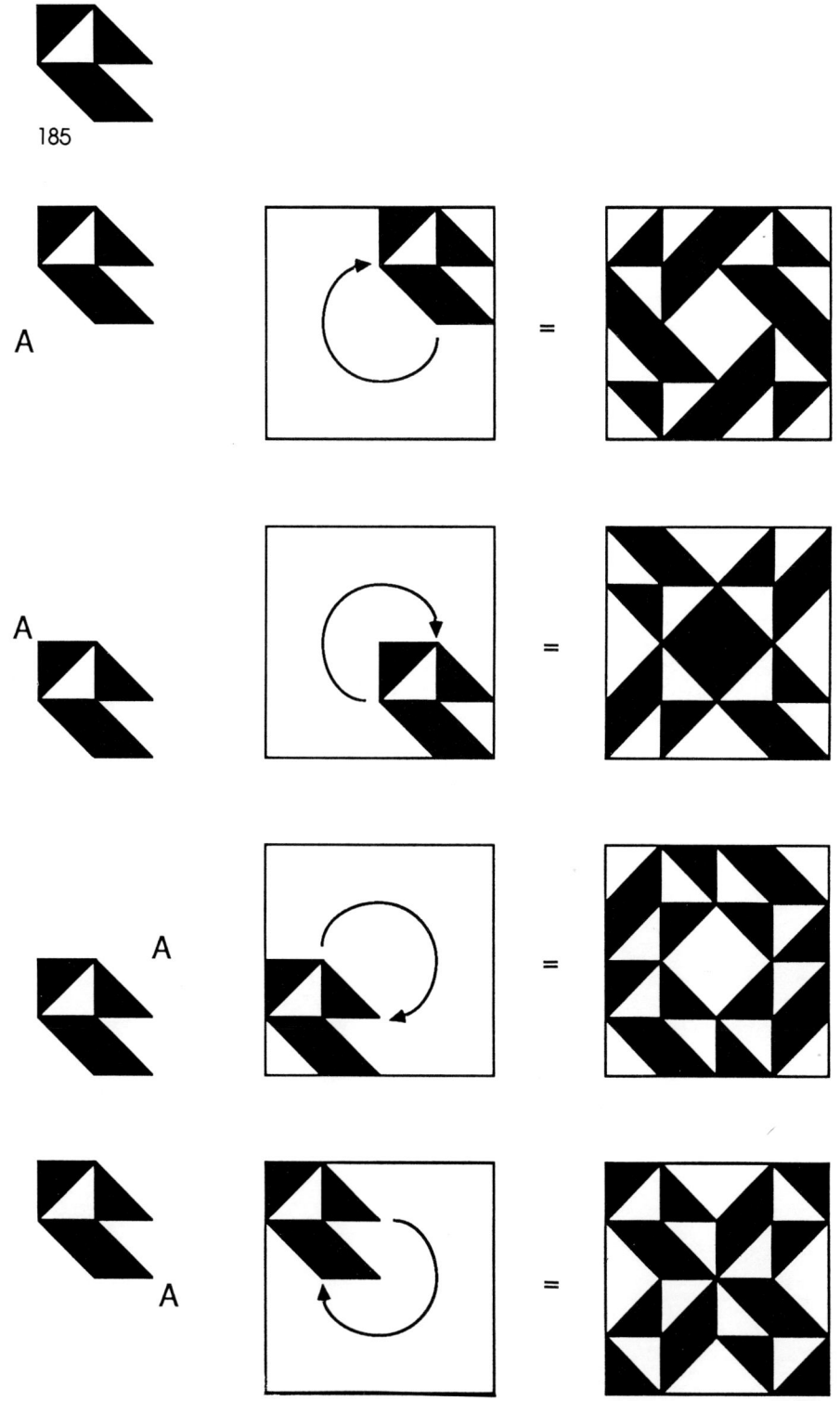

185

COLLECTION OF PILGRIM/ROY ANTIQUES
Devil's Puzzle Variation
78" x 84"

COLLECTION OF PILGRIM/ROY ANTIQUES
Barn Raising Variation
71" x 80"

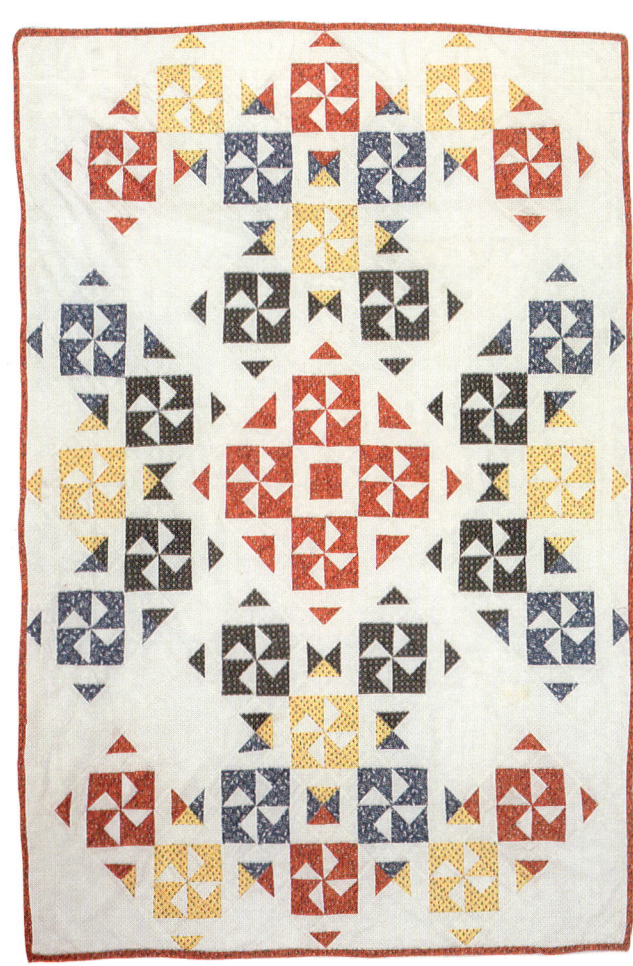

RUTH CHALLAND
Floating Pinwheel Tablecloth
42" x 63"

MARY WHITEHEAD
Pacific Flyway
60" x 78"

Rotation Around a Center Square You may also rotate the element around a center square. You may use a white square in the center or a black square.

White square   Black square

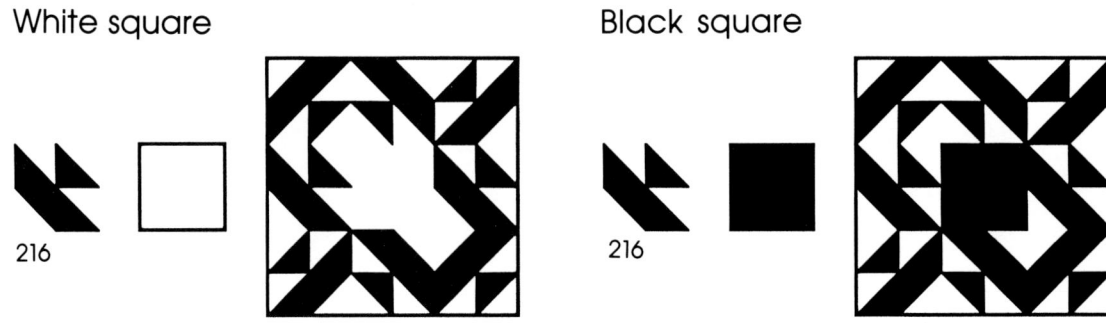

Using Two Elements Alternately rotate two different elements around a center square.

If you are working with graph paper and a pen, you will need to draw your element on a scrap of paper so you can physically turn it. It is very difficult to visualize the position of the element in its four orientations.

Rectangular Block You may also generate a rectangular block by drawing or stamping your element, then rotating the element 180° (turning it upside down) and placing it under the original element.

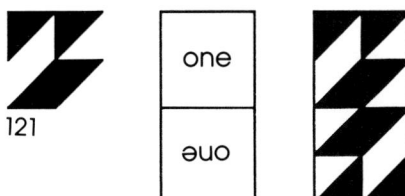

If you translate these rectangles on a rectangular grid, you will generate a striped pattern; and if you place them on a half-drop network, you will have a pattern with a strong diagonal bent.

Rectangular grid   Half-drop grid

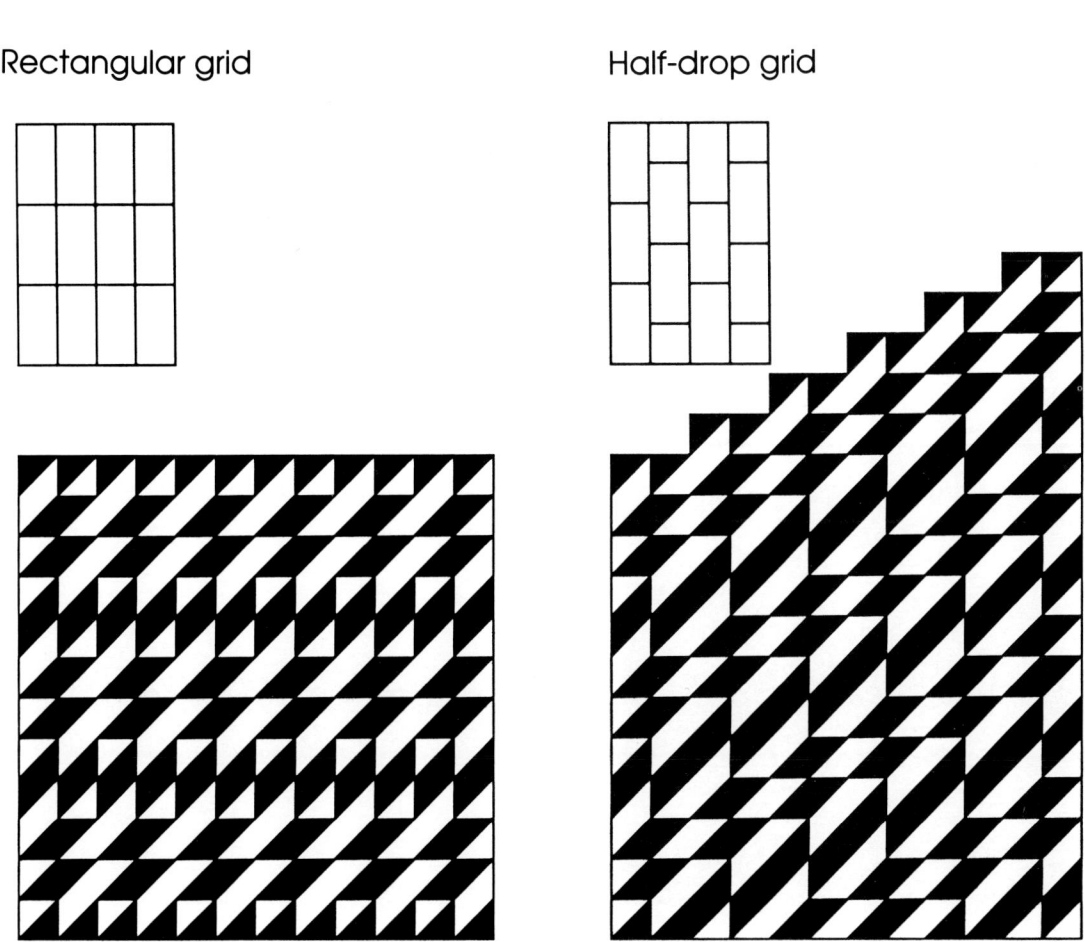

JENNIFER AMOR
Quick Patch Star Sampler
89"x 104"

SARAH BETH TENNISON
Bird Quilt
75"x 94"

BERYL SELF
Flowers & Baskets
53"x 53"

LINDA DENNER
Call Me Ishmael
39"x 33"

REFLECTION Reflection is the result of mirror imaging your design element. The easiest way to see these patterns is to place mirrors on two adjacent sides of your design element or through the middle at a 45° angle and look at the patterns at the point where the mirrors meet.

When you use the mirrors on your design elements, you will quickly see many different patterns. This is a fast weeding out process in which you need only record those patterns you like. You will discover many of your old favorite traditional blocks along with an infinite number of new ones which are in the traditional mode. These are the most restful patterns within the system. The more symmetry you have, the more balance and repose you have.

Holding the mirrors at a 90° angle.
The mirrors meet at point B in this example.

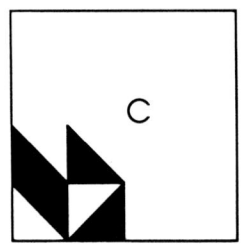 =    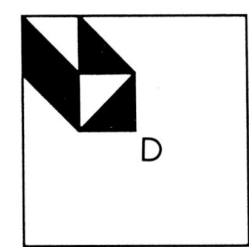 =

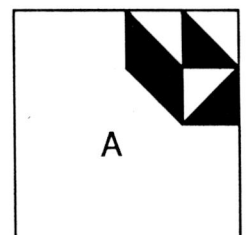 =

Holding the mirrors at a 45° angle.
One mirror is on AB the other on BD.

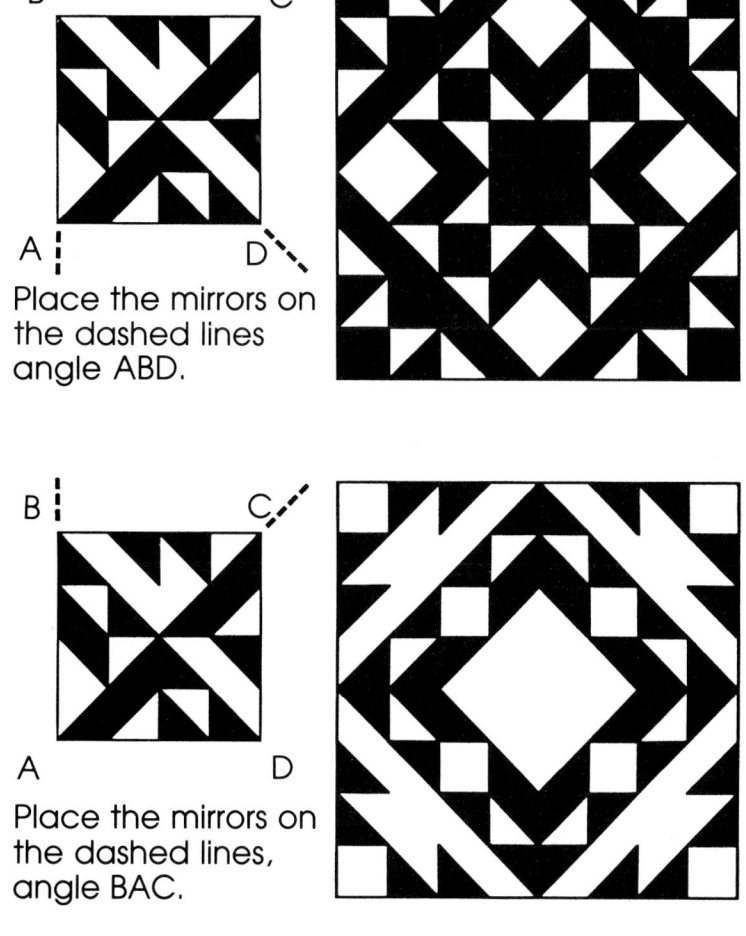

Place the mirrors on the dashed lines angle ABD.

Place the mirrors on the dashed lines, angle BAC.

Use two mirrors to find the other patterns that lie within. Look at BCA, ACD, CDB, BDA, DAC, and CAB.

COMBINATION   Once you have established a block pattern which you like, try it in combination with another block, either traditional or one you have discovered.

Another possibility is to reverse the coloring of the block you have chosen and combine with your original block.

Devil's Puzzle is an example of alternating your original block and the reverse coloring of your original block.

If you are working with a rubic's cube (see page 30), try combining it with a simple 9-patch block.

BORDERS   Try one of these six ways to generate border patterns.

Translation

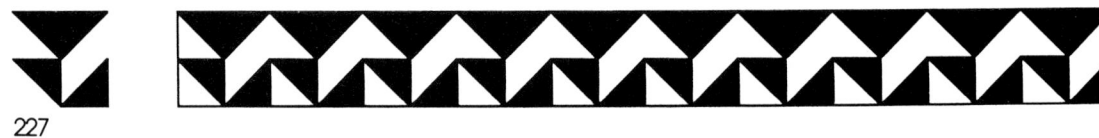

227

Rotation through 180°

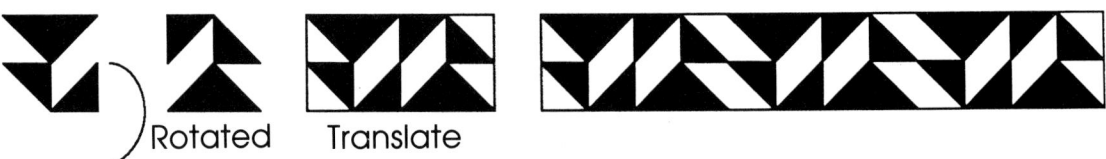

Rotated   Translate

Mirror reflection holding the mirror on the bottom of the element.

Translate

Mirror reflection holding the mirror on the right side of the element.

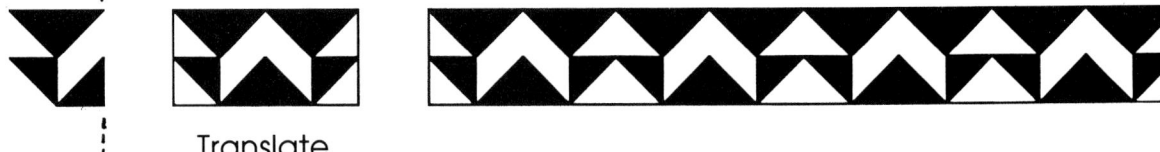

Translate

Mirror Glide Hold a mirror on the bottom of the element and bring the resultant mirror image beside the original element

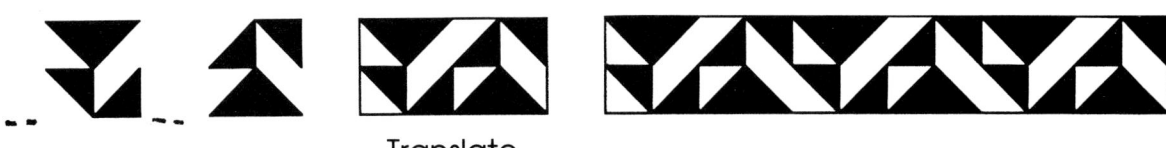

Translate

Mirror Reflection Hold mirrors on both the bottom and one side of the element.

Translate

RUBIC'S CUBE You may use a Rubic's cube to investigate the possibilities which occur when using nine permutations. There are 262,144 possible combinations using only two colors. You won't soon run out of possibilities, as you would have to record 20 of these patterns a day, 365 days a year, for 36+ years to document all of them.

To prepare your Rubic's cube, you peel off the colored plastic squares and cut them in half along the diagonal. Return one half to the cube, placing all of the half squares on one side in the same orientation. Each of the four sides around the cube will thus represent one of the original permutations. For the remaining top and bottom you may place the half squares at random or any way you choose. You then manipulate the cube and when you see a pattern which interests you, you would record it on graph paper or carve a stamp. (A four by four cube, Rubic's Revenge, is now available for exploring 16-patch patterns.)

Cut the plastic squares in half.

Manipulate the cube.

Record the pattern on graph paper.
(See page 32)

Or

With a carved stamp.
(See page 35)

The Rubic's cube allows you to explore 9-patch designs and many of these yield instant quilt blocks when rotated, forming a 36-patch design.

METHODS OF APPROACH

SUPPLIES: Graph Paper
           Pen

You may use graph paper, available in notebook form or by the pad, and a pencil or felt-tip pen. For discovering patterns, four, five or six squares to the inch is recommended, as any graph paper which is smaller (8, 10, etc. to the inch) is hard on the eyes and difficult to color. Expresso (bold point) pen by Sanford works well. It is inexpensive, long-lasting and readily available. It also comes in colors, though initially you should work only in black.

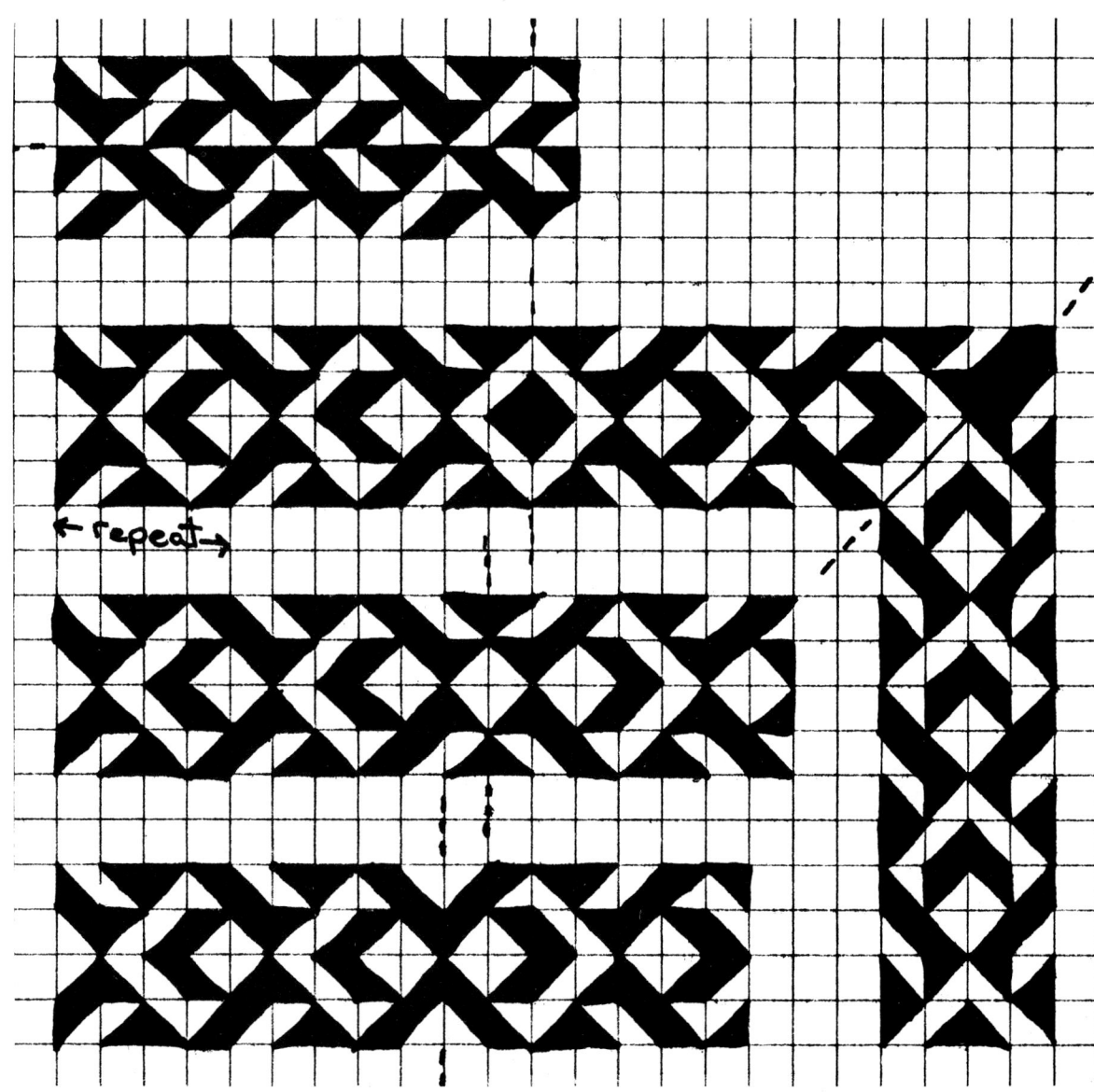

CARLENE CHANG
Red Shift
60"x 60"

JANET HARTNELL
Triangles #2
55"x 55"

The graph paper and pen method of recording patterns is my favorite. It is a form of meditation for me - exciting and soothing at the same time. As I block in the half squares, I concentrate on the pattern and stay open to what the shapes suggest. A playful mood persists. I feel a close connection with early quiltmakers who probably looked at their discoveries and named them in a similar fashion.

Working exclusively with pen and graph paper, however, can be restrictive. Because of the time involved, you will not be as quick to play around and manipulate the blocks just to see what might happen. It is also hard to visualize the overall pattern with only 4 or 6 blocks, but the time necessary to color in 30 or 40 may prove discouraging. On the following pages you will, therefore, find several other methods for discovering patterns which can be used in conjunction with graph paper and which, hopefully, will encourage you to play with the elements in search of new patterns.

Translation of Rubic's Cube + 9 Patch

Supplies: Erasers
Craft knife
Paper
Stamp Pad

CARVED STAMP

You may carve a rubber stamp from an eraser and stamp the patterns. If instant gratification appeals to you, then definitely try this method.

You may use several different kinds of erasers. The plastic erasers by Faber Castell are the easiest to carve, long lasting and will also give a good stamping. The art gum eraser, the cheapest, is also the most difficult to carve as it crumbles. The pink pearl eraser is also difficult to carve, not because it crumbles, but because it is made of a tougher material. It will, however, last a long time and stamp well.

The plastic erasers come in several sizes, but for the most economical use, the 1" x 2 1/4" is recommended. You cut the eraser in two 1" squares, draw graph lines on the eraser, color in the part you wish to remain and begin carving. You will need a craft knife. (X-ACTO is inexpensive and good.)

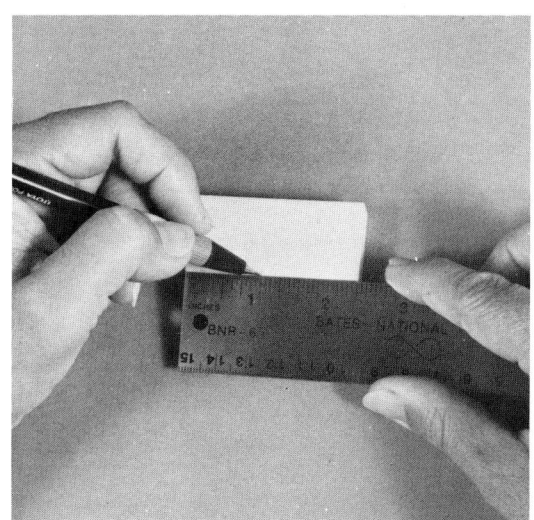

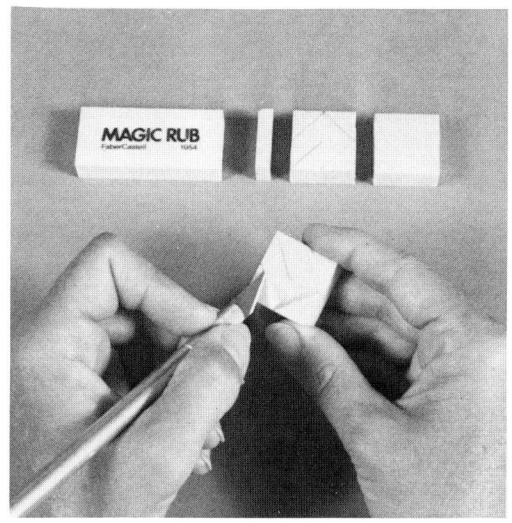

You hold the knife at about a 45° angle to give a beveled edge and cut along the lines indicated.

JEAN RAY LAURY
Stars & Stripes in Brown
51"x 51"

SARAH BETH TENNISON
Cube Lattice
41"x 41"

DORIS HOOVER
Lightening T's
85 1/2"x 85 1/2"

CARLA RODIO
CAROL SAMBORA, Quilted by Splendor
33"x 33"

You should then be able to lift out the part you wish to remove by putting the point of the knife under these cuts and wiggling it around. This will yield a stamp which is the mirror image of the element you selected (you will use this stamp in the exploration process). Now stamp this stamp on the other half of the eraser and carve as before, removing the uncolored sections. Voila! You now have a stamp of the original element and a stamp of its mirror image. Depending on the element chosen, you have two stamps which may represent from 1 to 8 different numbers on the key.

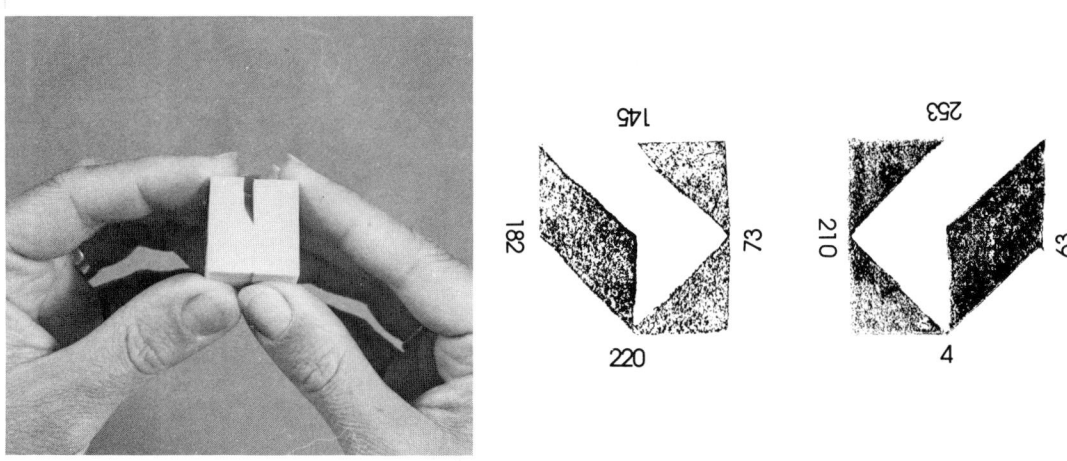

Stamping another stamp.

You may stamp with the eraser as it is or mount it with rubber cement on the bottom of an inexpensive plastic box. These boxes come in various sizes from 1" to 4" square. You may, also, mount 4 stamps on a 2" square box and stamp a page in minutes. Jane once stamped an entire 11" x 14" sketchbook in one evening with only two such stamps.

This method has other advantages besides speed. The stamping is generally a value of gray, and you can add other values or color without redrawing the design. It also reproduces well on copy machines if you want to try different colorways. Finally, you can use a textile paint or dye to stamp the pattern on cloth and create your own fabric.

Exploring some possibilities with these two stamps.

JOAN SCHULZE
Maui ©1982 Schulze
84"x 86"

JOAN SCHULZE
Oahu ©1981 Schulze
72"x 72"
Collection of R. Dakin,
International

LYN PIERCY
Raspberry Sherbert
88"x 101"

FABRIC   Supplies: Fabric in two colors
Scissors
Sewing Machine
Ruler
Grid

You may sew squares of half-square triangles and manipulate these to discover the patterns.

Construct the squares using the Quick Triangle method on page 54 in a size you usually work. (A finished 3" square is average.) You then lay the squares on a table, pin to a sheet, adhere to a flannel board, etc. -- whatever is most convenient in manipulating the squares to discover patterns. When you have discovered a pattern you like, you may record it on graph paper, carve a stamp or photograph it.

Rotation of element #176 starting on the left.

Completed rotation around a center square.

There are several advantages of working in this way. If you find a pattern you really like in the fabrics you have chosen, you may simply sew the squares together, and you are well on your way to a quilt. These squares are very helpful in getting a feel for the look of the block in its actual size. Sometimes, what seems coherent on the graph paper will look quite muddled when it is blown up and your eye is unable to take in the entire design at once. The graph paper is the same as viewing the design from a great distance or in a photograph, while the sewn squares will give you a better feel for the final design. As you make quilts using the Quick Triangle method, you can throw any leftover squares into your design pile.

Completed design rough

The pattern above is a reflection of the previous block. There are a lot of interesting things happening in it. Do you see the overlapping patterns and the diagonal, vertical, and horizontal reverse mirror images? Patterns within patterns. The overall appearance, however, is hard to take in all at once. Using this design rough as a starting point, what changes would you make to achieve a more cohesive look?

PATRICIA CAIRNS
Pinwheel
90"x 90"
Private collection

PATRICIA CAIRNS
Equinox
66"x 66"
Private collection

LINDA LILLARD
Aurora, the Dawn
61"x 61"

COPY MACHINE Supplies: Pen
Graph Paper (4 to the inch)
Scissors
Paste

You may construct a page such as the sample shown and make 10 or more copies at your local copier. Cut out the blocks, manipulate and paste them down when you have discovered a pattern you wish to record. You will get more elements on 5, 6 or 8 to the inch graph paper, but the blocks are so small they are difficult to manipulate and to paste.

Cut out all identical blocks.

Glue down the blocks in a variety of setting arrangements.

Make several copies of the pasted down page. Color each page differently to discover what possibilities exist.

MYRNA S. WACKNOV
H is for Harriet
36"x 54"

COMPUTER

A computer can be a lot of fun in designing patterns. The Apple Macintosh on which I'm working, with the addition of the MacDraw program, can do translation, rotation and reflection! Repeat copies of half square triangles or an entire block for that matter can be made just by pressing the mouse button or holding down two specific keys. Fabric patterns appear magically with a press of the mouse button. It's dazzling what it can do. However, it can also be frustrating. It takes longer than the ads suggest to master the machine and programs. Mistakes can be monumental. With a pencil you can't do much damage, a few squares at most. With a computer, you can vaporize an entire page with the press of a key. If you already have a computer or are buying one for another reason, see if software is available for doing geometric drawings. In addition to MacPaint and MacDraw for the Apple Macintosh, Random House has a program called Patchworks for the Apple II series of computers that works with half square triangles and squares. Not all programs work on all computers. Check out the programs and computers that are available to make sure that they are compatible.

There isn't anything you can do on the computer that you can't do with a pencil and paper and time.

Below are some of the functions of the MacDraw program for the Apple Macintosh computer.

248

Duplicate

Rotate left   Rotate right   Flip vertical   Flip horizontal

Background patterns can be added.

To make a rotation pattern, alternately duplicate, rotate, and position.

Translation is achieved by alternately duplicating and positioning the element.

To make a reflected pattern, alternately duplicate, flip vertical, or horizontal, and position.

LOGICAL BREAK-UP

Templates use a minimum number of piecing units. It is an economical system in that sense. Templates come in many shapes and sizes. Machine methods, to be efficient, need long straight seams. A grid underlies both template and machine piecing methods, but with machine methods the grid usually shows more strongly in the finished work. This is because odd shapes are broken down into smaller basic shapes often right triangles and squares. Squares are obvious enough, but triangles need some thinking about. Do you remember right triangles from schoolwork? A triangle with two equal length sides separated by a 90° angle. I thought I'd never use that bit of information! Now, I not only use it, I know there are two kinds. Where did I get this second kind of right triangle from, a right triangle that you won't find in any math book? I made it up!

Look at these triangles. No matter how you turn them, they stay the same. Yet in sewing we need to know which side will join first with another triangle. That is the distinction between half square triangles and quarter square triangles.

Half square triangles join along their long sides and are measured along their short sides.

Quarter square triangles are just the opposite. They join on one of their short sides and are measured on the long side.

I suppose we could say, "who cares", but knowing about quarter squares can sometimes save you some work. You can make your whole quilt out of half square triangles if you want. Quilters who don't know about quarter squares often do. If you don't have to go to all that trouble, you usually don't want to.

Look for ways to combine shapes in your quilt patterns. Place your design on a grid composed of squares. The vertical and horizontal lines of the pattern must be on the lines of the grid. Intersection points must also be on the grid. Usually this is enough to see how your quilt could be made. Often, however, shapes can be combined into larger construction units.

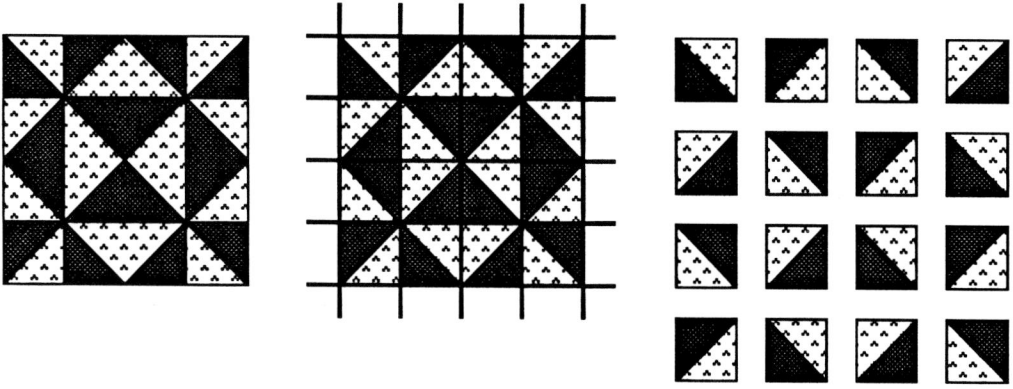

Let's look at this seemingly straightforward block again. Could we combine some areas? Is there more than one alternative to choose from?

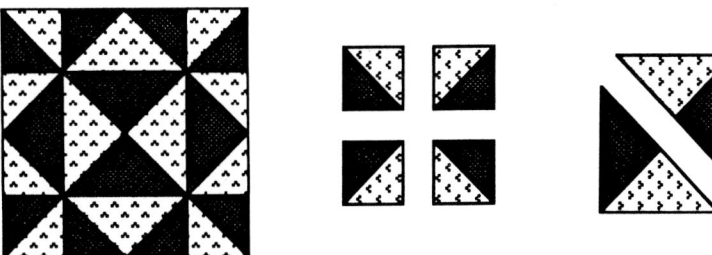

The center section looks promising. Instead of four half square triangle pairs, sew the large triangles of the dark fabric to the large triangles of light fabric. This would result in two sewing units instead of four.

What about the center side sections? Here we have three pieces. What are our choices? We could make two half square triangle units. Or we could quick mark the light half square triangles and the dark quarter square triangles. Sounds like a toss up.

   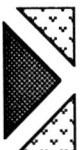

Did you notice the large half square triangles? Cock your head to the side and look at the block on the diagonal. What if you made large half square triangles in the center and filled in with small triangles on the outside? On the surface, it sounds easy; but remember, half square triangles are measured on the short side. The grain of your fabric would run diagonally through your block. This approach would trade a little convenience for the headache of diagonal blocks. Not a good solution!

That brings us back to all half square triangles or a combination of half squares and quarter squares. Let personal preference decide.

All half square triangles.
Fewer seams. More math.

METHOD OF SEWING

First decide what you will use as a measuring system. You have two choices. Each has its advantages and possible shortcomings.

Plastic Rulers You can do all of your measuring with one of the specially designed plastic rulers. The C-Thru Ruler Co. and Salem Industries are two sources for a variety of these rulers.
    These rulers are:
1. Small and therefore easy to handle.
2. Less expensive.
3. Potentially less accurate. Check the individual ruler you are considering buying for accuracy.
4. Less versatile. You are limited to the intervals marked on the ruler. Eighths of an inch are necessary, but many rulers only go as small as quarters.
5. Easily available.

Grid and Straight Edge I bought my grid at an architects and draftsman's supply store. It is a heavy plastic coated paper grid and absolutely accurate. It comes in different widths and is sold by the yard or fraction thereof. Using a T Square, I lined it up square on my table, then taped it down with a clear wide tape. My particular piece is 38"x 46". (This allows an entire yard of fabric to be worked at once.) On top of the grid is the cutting mat. It is 1/2" smaller than the grid on all sides. (It is not fastened down, but doesn't move.) My straight edge is metal (a yard stick). If using a grid and straight edge measuring system, you use the intervals on your grid and ignore any measurement markings on the straight edge and cutting mat.
    The grid and straight edge are:
1. More expensive to buy.
2. Potentially more accurate.
3. Can handle a full yard of fabric at once.
4. More versatile. You can work every measurement from 1/8" up to the maximum size of your grid rather than just the widths of your plastic strips or the intervals on your plastic ruler.

Scissors and Rotary Cutters You will need a quality pair of scissors such as Ginghers. Ginghers give you the option of cutting through many layers of fabric at once with ease.
Rotary cutters are an additional possibility. They seem to have been designed with machine piecing methods in mind. They can cut through several layers at once as well as allowing you to dispense with some marking as you cut along the edge of the straight edge. (Be careful, improper use of rotary cutters can result in severe cuts.)

HALF SQUARE TRIANGLES

You must understand the difference between the marking size and the finished size. It may not be what you think it is. With 1/4" seams there is a 7/8" difference between the marked size and the finished size, not a 1/2" as with squares.

If you will be making your entire quilt from the same size of Half Square Triangles, I suggest you mark in whole inches and finish in fractions. If other shapes will be used in your quilt, squares for example, you may make a decision based on what would be the easiest to do. Thus if you measure in whole inches, you will finish in fractions and the reverse is true also. If you measure in fractions, you will finish in whole inches.

For example:

Mark	Finish
4"	3 1/8"
3 7/8"	3"

MARKING

Once you have selected a method of marking and determined your marking size, you are ready to begin marking. Of the two pieces of fabric you will be using, mark the wrong side of the lighter fabric. For this example, I'll assume that you are making a quilt completely out of the same size triangles. Since they will all finish the same size, you might as well mark in whole inches and finish in fractions. In this example, you'll mark at 4" intervals.

Mark vertically and horizontally at 4" intervals.

If you need individual triangles for any reason, mark diagonally through the corners of the squares in one direction only. But if you want the triangles to ultimately be sewn together in pairs, USE THE FOLLOWING DIRECTIONS INSTEAD.

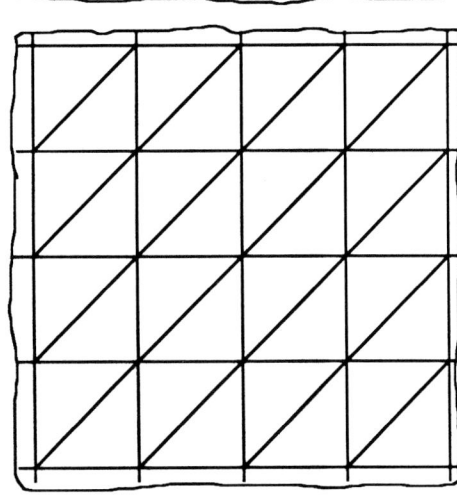

When you want to sew the triangles together in pairs, you need to mark sewing lines rather than cutting lines. These lines need to be a quarter inch from the center of the square.

Follow the pattern in the diagram for the greatest ease in sewing.

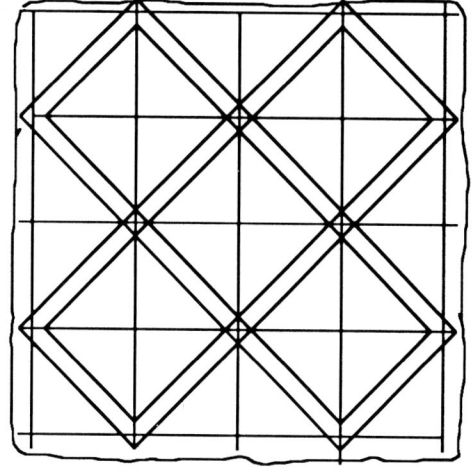

MARKING

Put the piece you have just marked on top of your contrasting fabric, right sides together. Pin in each triangle as shown.

Sew only on the diagonal stitching lines.

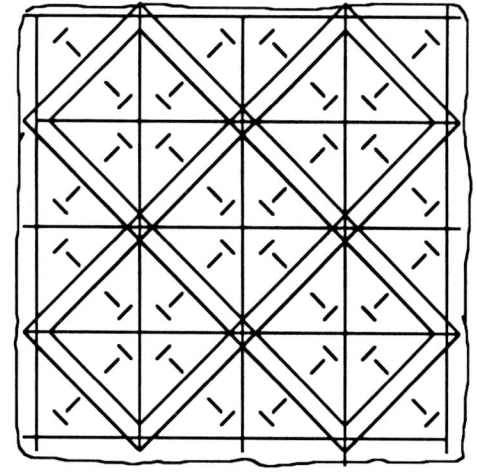

PINNING

SEWING

Cut on the horizontal and vertical lines. (You're cutting out squares.) Cut each square in half between the stitching lines.

Open triangles and press seams towards the darker fabric if they would show through your lighter fabric. Trim the triangle pairs. When a 1/4" seam is taken around all four sides, they will finish 3 1/8". You now have a stack of premade half square triangle pairs. They are now ready to make up in whatever pattern you have in mind.

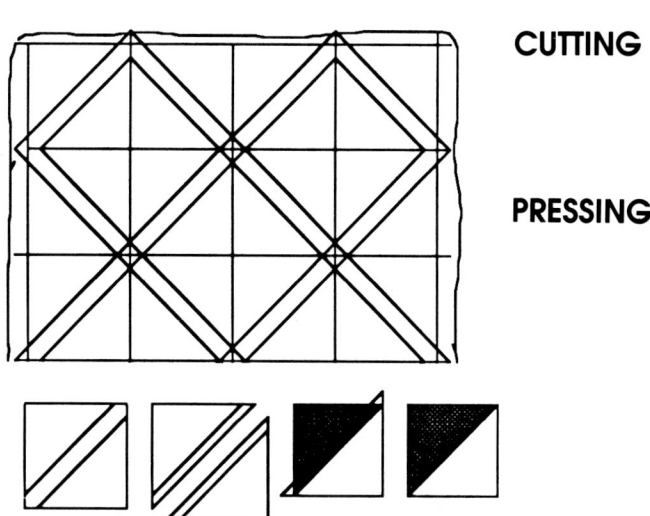

CUTTING

PRESSING

QUARTER SQUARE TRIANGLES

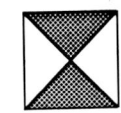

Quarter Square Triangles are similar to Half Square Triangles. They are the result of a square being divided into quarters.

Read through the instructions and then read again while using two practice pieces of fabric before going ahead with the project you have in mind.

Again, you must understand the difference between the marking size and the finished size. With 1/4" seams, there is a 1 1/4" difference between the marked size and the finished size.

Again, if you measure in whole inches, you will finish in fractions and if you measure in fractions, you may finish in whole inches. Decide which way to go based on what other shapes and sizes you will be making.

For example:

Mark	Finish
5"	3 3/4"
4 1/4"	3"

In the following example, you'll mark 5" and finish at 3 3/4".

MARKING

Of the two pieces of fabric you will be using, mark the wrong side of the lighter fabric.

Mark vertically and horizontally at 5" intervals. Mark diagonally in one direction.

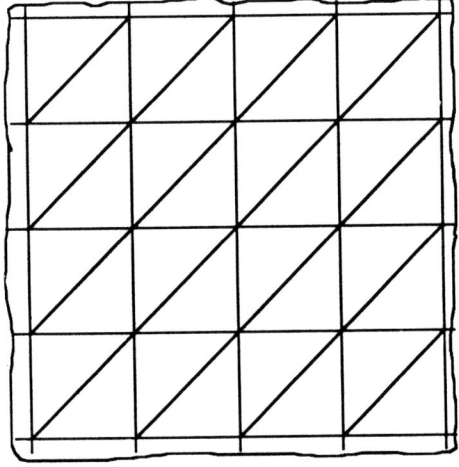

TO MAKE SINGLE TRIANGLES mark in the opposite direction also and cut out the single triangles. But if you want the triangles to ultimately be sewn together in pairs, use the following directions for marking.

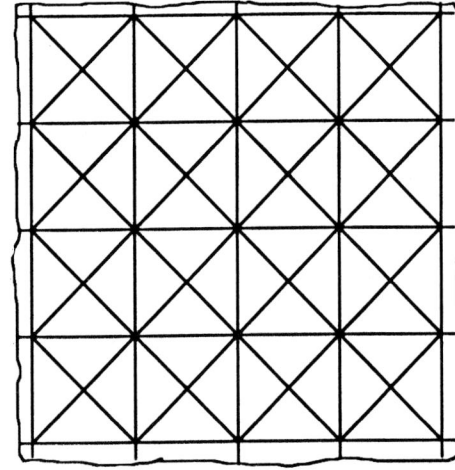

Working in the opposite diagonal direction, mark pairs of lines that are each a quarter of an inch from the center of the square.

Pin the piece you have just marked to your contrasting fabric, right sides together. This is to keep it from shifting while it is being sewn.

Sew on the paired diagonal lines that you have just drawn.

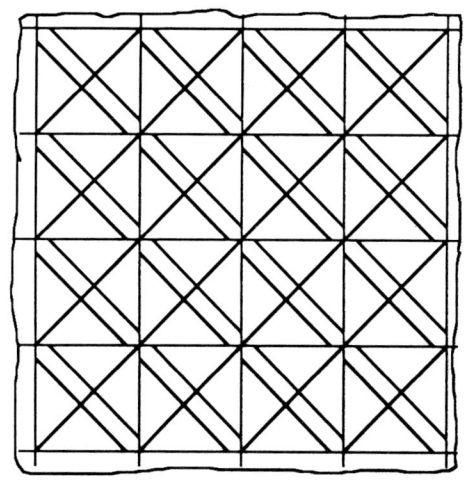

PINNING

SEWING

Cut on the vertical and horizontal lines. (You're cutting out squares.) Cut each square in half between the stitching lines. Cut on the single diagonal line.

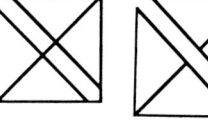

CUTTING

Open triangles and press seam allowances towards the darker fabric if they would show through your lighter fabric. Trim the triangle pairs. When a 1/4" seam is taken around all three sides, they will finish 3 3/4". You now have a stack of pre-made quarter square triangle pairs.

PRESSING

Note that the triangle combinations are of two types.

If you wish to have all of the quarter square triangle pairs be identical, follow one of these diagrams for marking and sewing.

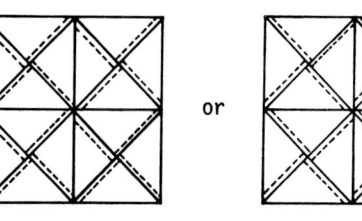

 or

57

DORIS HOOVER
Garden of Eden, detail
80"x 80"
Collection of Andy & Ginny Lewis

PATRICIA CAIRNS
Fireworks
96"x 60"

CARLA RODIO
Appalachian Trails #3
60"x 60"

CARLA RODIO
Appalachian Trails #2
60"x 60"

SQUARES 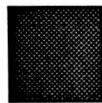 While we're working primarily with half square triangles, you might want to incorporate squares in your quilt. The following method is based on Seminole patchwork. With it you can cut out squares quickly or make rows of presewn squares. To make rows of presewn squares, you cut your fabric into strips. Sew the strips together and finally cut this unit apart into rows of presewn squares.

To begin, you need to determine the finished size of your square. For a 1/4" seam allowance, there is a 1/2" difference between the marking size and the finished size.

For example:

Mark	Finish
4"	3 1/2"
3 1/2"	3"
3 5/8"	3 1/8"

 Once you have selected a method of marking and have determined your marking size, you are ready to begin. Of the two pieces of fabric you'll be using, mark the wrong side of the lighter fabric. For this example, I'll assume you're making some nine patch blocks to alternate with a rubic's cube block. The half square triangles and the squares must be marked at different sizes to finish the same size. If we marked the triangles at 4" intervals to finish 3 1/8", we'll mark the squares at 3 5/8" to finish at 3 1/8".

MARKING Mark the wrong side of your fabric at 3 5/8" intervals. Mark in one direction only.

(FOR INDIVIDUAL SQUARES MARK IN BOTH DIRECTIONS AND CUT OUT.)

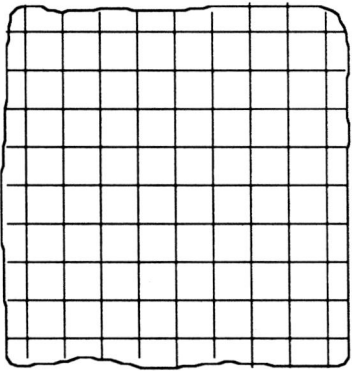

Following the lines you have drawn, cut the fabric into strips.

Mark and cut your other fabrics into strips.

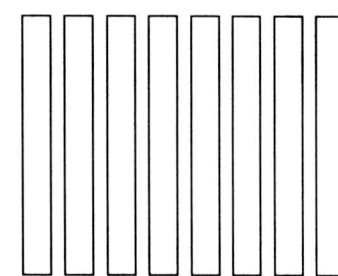 **CUTTING**

Machine stitch the strips together in groups of three. Use a 1/4" seam allowance. Two thirds of your strips are sewn together in this order; a dark strip, a light strip, and a dark strip.

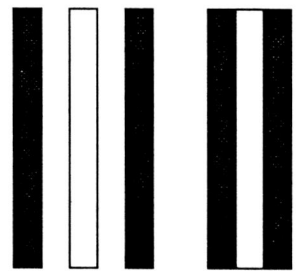 **SEWING**

The rest of the strips are sewn together in the reverse order; a light strip, a dark strip, and a light strip.

Press the seam allowances away from the light fabrics.

PRESSING

Mark crosswise at 3 5/8" intervals.

 **MARKING**

Cut the strips crosswise on the lines you have just drawn.

 **CUTTING**

Sew three combinations together to complete the block. Use a 1/4" seam allowance. It is easier to match the corners if the seam allowances lie in opposite directons.

 **SEWING**

If you have sharp scissors such as Gingher's, try marking one piece of fabric. Layer up to 8 pieces total with the marked piece on top. Layer in pairs right sides together. Carefully cut through all layers while the fabric is still on the board. Now peel off the top two and they are right sides together and the edges are even.

If you use a rotary cutter, use the same procedure, except you can dispense with the initial marking.

JEAN RAY LAURY
Four Square
84"x 84"

JOAN SCHULZE
Enchanted Hill © 1984 Schulze
68"x 74"
Collection of Mr. & Mrs. Chapman III

INSTANT GRATIFICATION

112

Translation

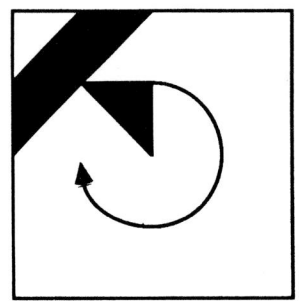

Rotation

Reflection

Translation

106

Translation

152

Rotation

Translation
152 rotated creates the same pattern as 106 above.

Rotation

216

Translation

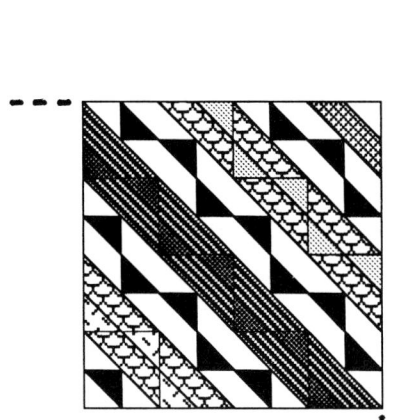

Reflection

Reflection

Rubic's Cube
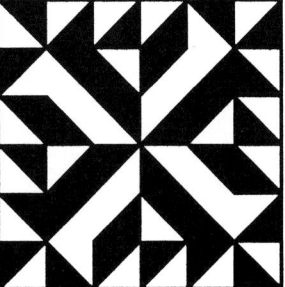

Rotation

Rubic's Cube

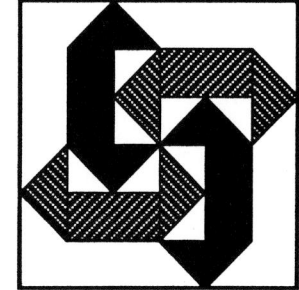
Rotation

9

10

Translation

Rotation

 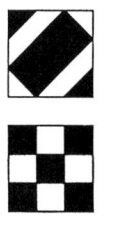 

Rubic's Cube
Nine Patch

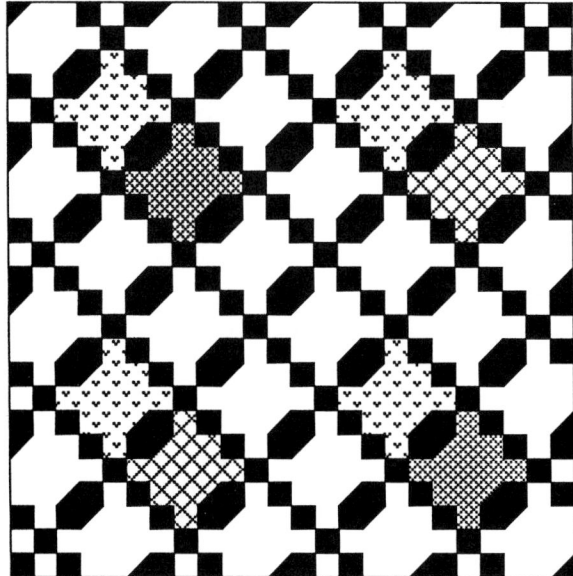

Translation

Reflection

249

254

Rotation around a center Square

182

Rotation

Translation

Translation of the original block and the reverse coloring of original block.

79

Translation

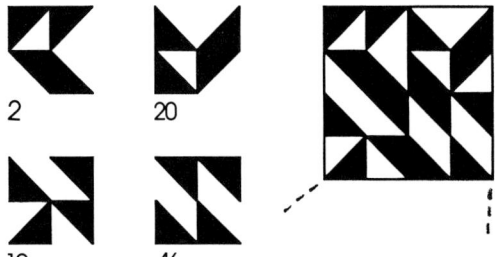

Reflection

Rotation

Rotation

Reflection

220

Rotation

A mess. Try Again.

  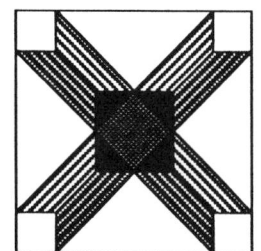 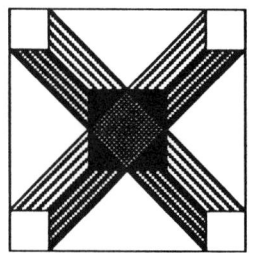

79   Rotation

 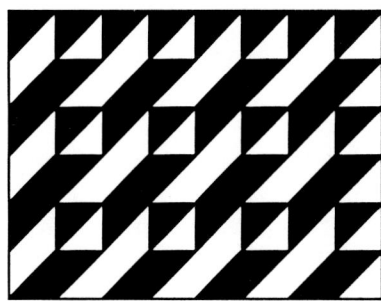

121

Translation

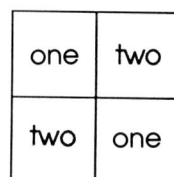

Rubic's Cube

Reflection

Translation

ARTISTS

Jennifer Amor
3702 Blossom St.
Columbia, SC 29205
(803)256-0146
Quick Patch Star Sampler, p 22
Quiltmaker, teacher specializing in quick piecing techniques, bargello patchwork and wearable art. Workshops, commissions, lectures.

Patricia Cairns
4424 West 2nd Ave.
Vancouver, V6R IK5, Canada
Pinwheel, p 44, Equinox, p 44,
Fireworks, p 58
Teacher, lecturer, sells her work.

Ruth Challand
Fletcher, NC
Floating Pinwheel Tablecloth, p 19.

Carlene Chang
Berkeley, CA
Red Shift, p 33,
Nikki's Quilt, back cover.

Linda Denner
108 Pine Street
Garden City, NY 11530
Call Me Ishmael, p 23
Writer, teacher, and lecturer

Janet Hartnell
733 West Mill
New Braunfels, TX 78130
Triangles #2, p 33
Sells her work and does commissions.

Doris L. Hoover
3505 Evergreen Dr.
Palo Alto, CA 94303
Lightening T's, p 37,
Garden of Eden, p 58
Teacher, lecturer, quiltmaker specializing in approaches to creativity.

Jean Ray Laury
Clovis, CA
Stars & Stripes in Brown, p 36,
Four Square, p 62,
Diamond Star, back cover
Writer, teacher, and lecturer; commissions and sells her work.

Linda Lillard
511 West Ohio Suite 100
Midland, TX 79701
(915)687-3232
Aurora, The Dawn, p 45
Lecturer and commissions and sells her work.

Lyn Piercy
San Francisco, CA
Raspberry Sherbert, p 41.

Paul D. Pilgrim
5380 Shafter Ave.
Oakland, CA 94618
Devil's Puzzle Variation, p 18
Barn Raising Variation, p 18
Teacher of traditional and original design and lecturer on Antique Quilts.

Carla Rodio
135 Circle View Drive
Hendersonville, NC 28739
(704)692-1971
Splendor, p 37
Appalachian Trails #3, p 59
Appalachian Trails #2, p 59
Teacher, sells her work.

Gerald E. Roy
5380 Shafter Ave.
Oakland, CA 94618
Devil's Puzzle Variation, p 18
Barn Raising Variation, p 18
Teacher on color and lecturer on Antique Quilts.

Joan Schulze
808 Piper Ave.
Sunnyvale, CA 94087
Maui © 1982 Schulze p 40
Oahu © 1981 Schulze p 40
Enchanted Hill © 1984 Schulze p 63
Teacher & lecturer; exhibits and sells her work and does commissions.

Beryl N. Self
Menlo Park, CA
Flowers & Baskets, p 23
Teacher.

Sarah Beth Tennison
Camarillo, CA
Bird Quilt, p 22
Cube Lattice Wall Hanging, p 36.

Myrna S. Wacknov
675 Matsonia Dr.
Foster City, CA 94404
H is for Harriet, p 48.
Fiber artist, currently working with an original process for making hand painted silk scarves; sells her work and lectures.

Mary Whitehead
1200 Belair Way
Menlo Park, CA 94025
Pacific Flyway, p 19
Teacher emphasizing traditional patterns.

OTHER BOOKS BY BARBARA JOHANNAH

CONTINUOUS CURVE QUILTING
by
Barbara Johannah
$8.95
56 pages

MACHINE QUILTING THE PIECED QUILT. A method of machine quilting pieced patterns that is adapted to the unique abilities of sewing machines. This technique is the equivalent of hand quilting -- quilt in the area you want, then move easily to the next areas without finishing off and beginning new threads. You accomplish this by quilting in gentle arcs through the corners to reach the next area to be quilted. This minimizes the number of starts and stops. This technique is ideal for quilting patterns that have a figure/background relationship.

"Barbara is an original thinker. She has given much of value to the present state of the art of quilting in North America. The book is worth every cent it costs." Canada Quilts

QUICK QUILTMAKING HANDBOOK
by
Barbara Johannah
$8.95
ISBN 934342-01-6
128 pages

Heavily illustrated with line drawings and photos.
Instructions for Quilts, Totes, a Garment, etc.
Covers the new method for fast and simple piecing that cuts the time to make a pieced quilt top down from months to days. The quality of construction remains unchanged, only the amount of time is reduced. First projects are recommended and are fully explained and illustrated for the beginner or the experienced quiltmaker. This is the complete how-to book with instructions included on planning the quilt, tools and equipment needed, yardage calculations and much more.

"The lady who originated one of the best short cuts to quilting in the 20th century.."
Ladies Circle Patchwork Quilts
"With Johannah's book you are set free to make a quilt in a weekend or two...downright mind blowing...Barbara's methods are brilliant." Open Chain

QUICK QUILTING Make a Quilt This Weekend
by
Barbara Johannah

Published in 1976 and no longer available. This first book on quick machine methods contained directions for making traditional patterns composed of squares, rectangles, triangles, and diamonds.

Quilts on the Back Cover

JEAN RAY LAURY
Quilted by CAROLYN GREER
Diamond Star
80"x 80"

CARLENE CHANG
Nikki's Quilt
42"x 47"
Collection of Nikki Wong

Barbara Johannah, P.O. Box 396, Navarro, CA 95463